HYPERFIXATIONS

BELINDA RODDIE

Copyright © 2023 Belinda Roddie

First paperback edition June 2023

*To my neurodivergent family, friends, and loved ones:
May you never be ashamed of your hyperfixations and passions.*

SO BE IT

You call them hyperfixations:
I call them lifelines,

the marrow coloring
my bones, the nourishment my body
requires before I enter the lion's den
(which includes a whiteboard
and many, many desks).

I call them
the finest mythology I've read,
and the crispest mead
I've had the pleasure to sip.
They are the mornings

I spent waiting for dry bread
to save my spirit,
and the nights I've lingered

on the phone with a lover's arms
draped like a shawl across my shoulders,
telling me it's time to forget today. But
I cannot forget these obsessions

when they leave a direct impression,
reminding me to take breaths
in between sticky meringue kisses
because this heart of mine can

never. Slow. Down.
And this mind of mine will

never. Ever. Stop.
And this soul of mine

will find time
after each panic attack
to turn search histories
and broken coffee cups
and random fits of textual passion
into something Extraordinary

into something Spectacular

into something remarkably
similar to Love.

INDULGENCE

SPHYGMOGRAPH

can you feel my pulse
against your pulse
feeding into other pulses
pulsing outward
outward
outward
into infinity?

are my veins swollen
like your veins are swollen,
and have we tapped into a vein
full of gold, or will we asphyxiate
in each other's arms like trapped
miners who appreciate the drama?

I have always been told
that my heart rate is lower
than normal.

But you make the percussion
run a marathon in sweats
and the perspiration
becomes a waterfall
and the waterfall
fills a reservoir.

And I drink from that pool
and am nourished for another
day, so pinch my wrist
and make sure I'm alive
for you, and you, and only you.

THE HUMAN CHANDELIER

The pearls drip off her one by one,
crackling as they peel from her neck,
her puckered skin - rough, raw,
and rosy. The maid sweeps
them up and collects them
in a silver bucket.

When you are alone with her, you'll smell
the rich molasses of her perfume, the
factory odor of her nail polish, brick
dust, lifted up, serving as her blush, her
rouge, her veil of stars.

They offer champagne in monoliths
at her estate. She waits for tea
and cake and sweetness on a silver
plate. Below the balcony, we play croquet
and wait for our hostess to tumble down,
down, in a cascade of precious stones,
glittering in a thousand weeping pieces.

HONEY

The simple teaspoon slips
from your fingers
directly between my lips.
So sticky.
Yet somehow, not as sweet
to me as sugar. Astounding.

The silverware is cradled
against my teeth like a rowboat
bobbing along a rocky sea.

I press my tongue upward
and embrace the tang.
Your hand makes it to my chin

and your fingers trace
the outline of my jaw
until they reach
the sunken ships of my eyes.

DEAR SOUS CHEF

Whaddaya say
we try some new recipes
out when it comes
to eating the rich?

I'm quite a fan
of rotisserie billionaire,
though good ol' fashioned
barbecue is always nice.
Taste the ribs!

Some of them are better
pan seared, but I wouldn't
bake any of the one percenters
in the oven - it leaves quite
a nasty lingering smell.

Still, we may as well
experiment with different seasonings
and condiments - garlic salt
and paprika are two of my faves
to sprinkle atop an oligarch's carcass.

This meat is far too fancy
to be served with ketchup
and should definitely not be
cooked any more than medium rare.

Serve 'em with sides of gorgonzola
mashed potatoes and fresh seasonal
vegetables. And now, a toast
to post-capitalist cuisine - rebellion
has never tasted so damn good.
Bon appetit!

MY FAVORITE SMELLS

Just before the rain kisses
concrete lips with sealed consent

and after the heat has dissipated
from crème brûlée and peppermint tea.

Right as the garlic sizzles perfectly
against the broccoli in the shallow pan

while like old friends, chocolate and cinnamon
dance in the kitchen, holding hands.

The moment your hair has dried from its latest
shampoo and I bury my face in the maze

it provides, I feel, at last, as if all positive
memories are lifted and cradled in wicker baskets.

Smell is hardly used in literature, and yet, when
the spine of a new book squeaks and creases,

I am reintroduced to the days of libraries as
a child - carpet, paper, and freshly baked words.

A TASTE

in the latest heat wave, she leaves
fingerprints on my skin
deep divots
in my swollen ankle
these tattoos are nearly permanent

I don't even remember the last time
I traveled over ten miles to anywhere

I only remember
that you wanted to go to the farmer's market
for peaches
and nectarines
counting all the seeds
as if they were the freckles
on my sun spotted cheeks

above us, we see two moons
if we squint and tilt our heads
at ninety degree angles
is it all right
that we pretend we can
see double?
or does that defy anything?
or anyone?

the greatest adventure
we could ever have right now
is wrapping ourselves up in a ball
underneath our bed
for monsters to play with

that way, our dreams retain
some semblance of wandering

DINNER AT MIDNIGHT

We forgot to eat until
the early morning's fingers
had simmered across our bare
bellies, and now, we were hungry.

So we served up a feast for our
weary souls: Spicy and sweet,
salt and cayenne pepper, leftover
sushi and tacos and brand new
chocolate bars and freshly boiled pasta.

We kissed with lips stained
with salsa and sauce and syrup
and lay on the couch together
with our stomachs distended
toward the stars.

Satisfied, we slept without
blankets, waiting for Lady Digestion
to visit and see the party guests out,
saving only the best for spare rooms.

I'm thankful we can host a banquet
for two from time to time, and
if we could afford it, we'd drink
rich wine in golden goblets, toasting
to a future less fraught with mortal fear.

FLAVOR COMBO BREAKER

Mint and seaweed are odd companions
and wouldn't be expected to go together,
but after dinner and a deep toothbrushing,
they're lying on their backs in a sea-wrapped
bed, holding hands and whistling.

It's almost too much to ask that my mouth
be freed from the burden of today's appetite,
replaced instead by the mild perfume of lips
held firmly against my own. Lips taste like
rose water and lavender - hard to catch in
baking, but sweet enough to make me levitate.

And I know I could drink the salt in the sea,
but the dehydration would be too much for me.
Don't expect a three course meal after what
went down at dinner last night: Instead, I'll
provide us a place to sit, a glass of wine, and
a nibble of something more tantalizing than sex.

POETIC CANNIBALISM

I'd like my heart ripped out
of my chest, please - toasted,
deep fried, and served back to me
with a garlic aioli drizzle on top
and some coleslaw on the side.

I'll eat it with a helping of mead,
just to settle my stomach
after consuming what I foolishly
believed to be a failed love affair.
But digesting that would require

scooping my brain out of my skull
like ice cream - and I'm not really
in the mood for dessert.

HOW ABOUT DESSERT?

This slice of heaven
is rich and heavy with cream.
It sits clumsily in the stomach,
pinning its consumer to the floor with
its weight, making digestion feel
more like purgatory than celestial
paradise. In fact, I don't think

I can finish the piece you've cut
for me. It's as big as my head, in
the awkward shape of a crude halo,
and the cake itself is so dry. The
sponge has been wrung out, and the
angels eating it with me have all
lowered their mouths into white

porcelain basins. When they reemerge,
their tongues are clotted with their
own inner vapors, and their teeth
are no longer pearls. And come to
think of it, it's so hot in here that the
frosting is starting to slide like
an avalanche down the side of my
plate, while you stab me in the neck
with the buttery tines of my own fork.

DOUGH FINGERS

The powdered flour orgasm in my
mouth is from your hands. Your speckled
sugar hands, the skin puckered from
the citrus grip of the whisk, my tongue
seeking out the creeks of flavor that
stain everything, from your thumb
to your crooked, sticky pinky.

You don't know when
to quit. You won't close
the recipe book just yet. You'll stir
me up like buttered egg yolks, eyes half-
melted in a bowl, salty residual urges
still pulsating against the mixer. I want
to lick it clean. I'm sure that
you'll reluctantly let me suck the batter

off the steel. There'll be cookies,
brownies, cakes, towering titans of
gladiator goodness frosted pink. Your
heaving chest, and iced nose, will remind me
that this is just one night, one result, out of
many, many more. And I will always ask
for second helpings, savoring each little spot
of sweetness that lingers
just above your upper lip.

BLUE-EYED DATES

Up, behind the
lock jawed pub faces sharing soggy fries and
pomegranate beer, you can see the faint
cerulean lamp lighting as we settle into a
sharp-edged conversation with our
neckties askew.

Hold on - I'm leaking snark from the
tooth-braced lip of my Irish lifeline
in the form of cider. Here's my
smartass card. Be sure to
punch a hole in the final checkbox so
I can get a free hot chocolate at the
local Upturned Nose Café.

No, you don't get to
pay the bill for my anecdotes.
They're cheap and they make
smoke buzz beneath everyone's
eyebrows. No one's bound to
flee these borders because the
White Russian ambiance is so
inviting. The Kahlua makes me
hum. Hazel and aqua flicker.
Iris meets iris. Starch high.

CANVAS, AS I LIVE AND BREATHE

You said to me once
that you wanted to leave
a lasting impression on both
my body and my soul. Well,
you've certainly outdone
yourself on the former: The acid

etchings are a marvel. Mad
kudos for the tattoos woven into
tangled sleeves on my biceps
after one swallow too many
of hot liquid fire. More curious,

however, is what you've burned
on my insides: Words and pictures
scrimshawed on my sternum,
echoes of cave carvings
on every bar of my ribcage.

When I drink water now, I feel
the chill that you imprinted on
the trembling tissue of my throat
and the coiled pulse of my esophagus.
I cannot eat anything anymore
without tasting you first. I was okay

with this, with the tea leaves stained
into my spine. With the whittling
of both our words, embedded in my
flesh like starry specks of flint. With
the obligatory, "It's not you, it's me,"
permanently painted under my eyelids,
so when I close them, I am forced
to dream about your final goodbye.

ENNUI

I gotta admit: there are a lot of ways
I can navigate the malaise of my brain.
My wife gave me a few ideas for this
stream-of-consciousness meter and rhyme.

"You can never write enough
about puppies," she said.
And she's right; they are quite adorable.
But the spiders in my cerebral cortex
have made quite a home in just an hour or so.

"Well, how about a bear and a boar
who are friends?" my wife asks. And sure,
I could do that, too. Two beasts frolicking
across the fantasy genre plains would do
nicely for a sweet poetic saga. But alas,

I'm tired, and I feel broken, and I know
all the pieces can be salvaged, but I've
had plenty of instances in which my actions
have been misinterpreted because, ironically,
I can't communicate with my muse even using a bullhorn.

So here are my words, for whatever they're worth.
And I didn't write about puppies or bears or boars.
Just about me, of course - poets are inherently
self-centered, but that's only because
no one else would dare write about them.

THIS EVENING IS ENOUGH

cloud over the moon
kissing its white forehead
letting misty palm linger
on a burning, pockmarked cheek
this is the time of night
when the fever normally breaks

moon cradles cloud
uses its curved body as
a makeshift bed, its craters
places to hide its hands
brings its knees up for support
and says that it's okay to cry

and when the tears come
the rain wipes the pavement
of gray and turns it white
the chalk melts into rivers
down a busy pedestrian sidewalk

you and I cover the asphalt
with our shadows, stretched
out by the row of lamp posts
rainbows don't come out after
the sun's set, but the storm brings
color to our faces, and that's enough

LORE

WELCOME BACK, CLASS (2021)

I will not play the role of martyr for you today.
I will not have my face cast in bronze, my photo

distributed like sticks of gum among the hungry flash bulbs
craving more than just a burst of light - a burst of flavor.
Something to literally chew on. Something to cry about.

Do not engrave a hero's title on the plaque of my headstone,
or sing schoolyard songs as you scatter my ashes. You
had the choice: To protect me, or to entomb me.

You chose the sarcophagus. It is far from ornate.
It contains the bones of an educator who will have died
from being forced into a net woven with strings of plague.

It will be nestled beside other unmarked skulls -
catacombs, fie you - belonging to those I taught,
and those I tried and failed to keep safe.

The blood we've sprayed from our lungs is not on
our hands, but yours. May you take the part of
Lady Macbeth if I am to be Duncan, slaughtered

for your crown, as you wash your hands over
and over again to get the stain out and bemoan the fact
that your hand sanitizer can eradicate the germs,
but not your own self-portraiture of malice.

SON OF PONTUS, PRIMORDIAL

I was actually born yesterday:
dredged from the water like soggy
flour, driftwood reshaped into a new
Pinocchio. Got a kiss on the nose
from a princess in purple and grew
flesh right in the middle of
the town square. I think I may
have scared the dogs and the children.

The way you smiled at me when you
took me into your cottage was alarming
and foreign. You scrubbed down my new
body with sheep's fleece, dressed me in
your father's tunic and robes. You taught
me all the words that would help me survive
in the middle of a storm. And after a few
hours, once the sun had set, you asked me
what I wanted my name to be.

It was simple, really: I had a list ready.
I was Aadi and Ashur and Genesis; I was
Navin, Neo, Nysa, and Dawn. Zora,
Aurora, Zerlinda and Zelenka -
Dagny and Digian, both of which
I had soft spots for. But you found another
sewn into my melting stitches: the last

anatomical spot where I was never fully
human. You touched the patchwork and
said to me, "I think Vivaan suits you. You
emerged from the sea with the sun caught
in your thatch roof hair." And I suppose
it fit, and you fit well with me, for your
name was Ordell, and we began this
new, warm, brazen life together.

DAUGHTER OF PASIPHAE

How did you feel, love, when I found
the lipstick drawn in mazes on the bathtub
like labyrinths dragged across the tile
until they melted into crimson wax
against the Minotaur's smile? Did

you find comfort in the color, in the
temporary tattoo? Did it tickle your
fancy to see your cosmetics staining
the rudimentary body of the basin,
which lifted its pelvis upward on clubbed
feet, limping its way to the nearest wall?

Art is meant to be seen, and this femme
display brings back your father's migraine.
What would he say to this, this modern
canvas left to suffocate with crushed carnauba
congealing in its mouth? Or did you, perhaps,
want him to find it, too, much to your sense
of humor - much less to your mother's
sense of shame? Crete be damned.

I did not wipe away the offending
residue until you had a chance to
admire your masterpiece. Your hair
still wet from the kitchen sink. Your hands
soft like clay after so much scrubbing
against running water. You wore mascara
like curtains over your face, only
drawing them apart for the occasional
first act of tears that threatened
to compromise your personal
cabaret. You left beads on the carpet, so

I could step on them and make them pop
like little plastic planets disrupted in their
orbit around a Holbein sun, its red and gold
rays stretched outward like a scarab beetle
stuck on its back and exposing its belly to
an uncaring world. You sketched
portraits in eyeliner on your

arms and legs, the vessel dipped in black
like charcoal, charred horns and ebony
bulls leaving scattered hoof prints, like
lust, fading against your own calves
and knees. Yes, I am sure you felt great

pride when I found the lipstick drawn
in mazes on the bathtub. Your brother
the beast sleeps in its enameled maw.
I look away from its dreams and seize
the golden thread that leads me from this
labyrinth, where by the cold and narrow
entrance, you already wait for me.

VULCAN'S CHILD

Your face was forged from fire:
your smile is too hot for me to
touch. I'd strip the layers of iron
from your skin if they didn't strip
the skin from my unsteady fingers.
You were born from an angry anvil,

the hammer that shaped your body
doing nothing to temper your ragged
soul. You burned the whole place
down and let the blacksmith swallow
the smoke of his own creation and
destruction. At long last, you found

the armor that fits your flesh best.
It fastened itself to your own steel
sternum. Your rib cage ached from
the weight of your heart. Valves
forcing flames through arteries
hollowed from the skeletons of
older swords and tanks and cannons,

their tongues and swollen lips melted
and reformed into your apparatus. In
another universe, you would be
a sculpture for the gods. Hephaestus
would have held you to his chest and

made you feel love. Quiet, warm love.
The kind that softens your sharp
and forbidding angles, your corners,
your gears that make your eyes blink,
your hair stand on end, and your laugh
ring like the chime of a clock tower
forcing the hour upon my little world.

COURTSHIP

Here, men serve their purpose,
and women serve their purpose, too.
They open their bodies up like drawbridges,
so when all's lowered, all suns rise,
and all moons are full, and all stars glisten
for the night of reverie, before everyone
needs to retire to their beds.

Here, spires rise in phallic sins,
and valleys dip in similar trespasses,
but in the private chamber, I kiss all
dips and curves in flesh and bends in bones,
for lovers' frames differ in the light of crisis.
I am willing to consummate dreams of all sizes.
If only they could all survive.

Here, I cry along the windows' lips and teeth.
Their fangs rise to meet my skin - how violent!
The night they protect is fragile behind sharp points.
Now, I must navigate my responsibilities as queen.
For kings have been dead for years on end,
and thank God for that, for my blood is stronger
than theirs. My blood carries words heavier than gold.

Here, I am desperate for love. And when I
descend by thin rope to wet ground, I feel the
rain sting my back as if it were nettles. Lord!
If only I were born in a different time! But alas,
now, I am lost in storms coated in sweetness,
hail leaving divots in too soft of flesh,
spots where I've served my purpose all too well.

WATERLOGGED

Mother, take me back
before I drown in the river Styx. My body
is heavier than the bricks of the church
where you have consigned your bones
before the flesh has even melted off.
Take me back. I beg you.

I am hungry for more than moss. I am
thirsty for more than ice. I want to sleep
to the sound of a lullaby, not
dogs barking and snapping
at my lonely ankles. Kharon threw me
overboard, despite the coin I provided.
Perhaps it was counterfeit after all.

Watch your husband add record numbers
to his company's profit, while your daughter
is submerged in saltwater and dances
in an algae woven skirt. He sells the brine

but won't pump it from bedraggled lungs
gasping for something sweeter,
sweeter,
damn it, sweeter.

Why can't I taste the caramel
swirling in the chocolate anymore? And why,
when I call you, does the dial tone
keep singing its song without vocal cords,
endlessly?
Endlessly?
Endlessly?

This family is waterlogged - soaked
and pruney all over. These new lifelines
are too short to bother with. I will die
with Hades hovering over my shoulder. You
will die, Mother, with the talisman of a false god
tucked in your withered cleavage. Faded,
decaying, and never, ever dried
in the sun.

CROWNED THRALL

She was a viking queen
who claimed me for herself,
and as we drank from steins, she rubbed
her hand across my knee. I couldn't
help but shiver.

Her hair was tied in braids -
more auburn than bright red, it
rose to face the winds
of our longboat as they rowed.
I would not touch an oar, she said:
I'd touch her, her alone.

She took me to her bed,
and instantly, the games began.
I sang a song for her, and in
return, she kissed my lips.
We weren't a secret here, not in
the middle of the ocean. And once
we conquered land, then I
would gladly be queen with her.

VELVET MANE

So you're thinking about leaving
the Regal Lioness for a better queen? Well.
Better pack your bags and head up
the mountain, because the only beast
nobler than the one you have is God.

She is so refined, surveying the domain
that you once shared; now you argue
and say, "It was rightfully mine." Her
crown is all burnish, but you'd reduce
its shine with your fake smiles, burning
the love lines on both palms until the scars
have withered all sense of fate away.

The Regal Lioness is not kind
to those who wrongfully wrong her.

Find all your sins staring through window
bars. Each kiss pulls you closer to
her guillotine, closer to the edge of the cliff,
closer to where you'll lose all sense of time.
You held royalty in your arms; the purple
between Heaven and Earth isn't radiant
enough for you? Foolish sovereign.
Her throne is much too good for you to perch on.

You will not find a more divine monarch than her.
Your endless quest for something better
leads to a broken grail with no lips to drink from.
And once you hold the shards in your hands,
you'll feel the sting of claws and teeth
on your shoulders and back: Not from the
queen, but from the members of her pride.

Friends of the Regal Lioness are not kind
to those who wrongfully wrong her.

THE DEER HEAD LODGE

There's never a vacancy at the Deer Head Lodge,
but I visit my lover there every Wednesday night.
She's lived in the same room for eight years or so,
and she doesn't mind not having a kitchen. She always

has champagne in the mini-fridge, and she always
serves it in a big silver bucket of ice, and she
always toasts to the new year, even when it's
Monday, January the second. Once the carbonation's

settled in our stomachs, she turns on the TV, but
she reads a book while the local news plays. The
star anchor is young and blonde and beautiful. Her
lips are like red sailboats floating
on an endless brown sea.

The Deer Head Lodge has a grille and bar,
and my lover can afford every entree and cocktail
on the menu. Her father's inheritance could have paid
for a house, but she prefers the rough intimacy

of a hotel room. Sheets that weren't meant
for just us now coil around my ankles and leave
me smelling like her: Rib-eye steak and steamed
broccolini, scallops and spilled Merlot, lychee
martinis and tiramisu. And sweat.

Every Wednesday night is the same: We eat
at the grille, we drink champagne, we fuck,
and we read novels together while the news
anchor recites the latest headlines with those red lips.
There's never a vacancy at the Deer Head Lodge,

though I wonder if it's because, like my lover,
there are people in these rooms who bury themselves
under the covers, shut the blinds that now conceal
the outside world, and never want to check out.

VACATIONING ON LESBOS

How much, Sappho, does Aphrodite
owe you after all your words and praise,
your contributions to the lyric genre -
simple, sweet, yet mellifluous? Does she

pay you royalties, offer you checks written
out on olive leaves? Or bottles of wine pulled
from the sweaty breast of Dionysus, who
hoards each vessel like a lush in a loincloth?

Does she steer her dove-yoked chariot
round to your island, her feet soaked in
the salt of the nearby sea, her hair still damp
from the foam that birthed her? You dictated

her words, that humble promise: "She that
fain would fly, she shall quickly follow. She
that now rejects, yet with gifts shall woo
thee. She that heeds thee not, soon shall

love to madness." Did she ever realize
that she was the one you wished to see
succumb to drought of sanity, leaving
her father's house of gold to sleep in

your arms as your fingers tremble
against your aging stylus? Come, now,
Sappho: this goddess owes you more
than tokens and verbal comfort. You must

kiss her gracious Vision, dear, while she
weaves her wiles into your heart like
Arachne's defiant silk upon the loom.
She must avoid slaying your spirit -
instead, she is bound by Zeus to subdue it.

THE WOBBLY MAN

The wobbly man can't help
dancing when he walks, and
he speaks every language when
he talks. He strings morning glories
across homes with two stories
and drinks honeysuckle out of a box.

When he can't decide on
which hat to wear, he sports all
of them at once; he doesn't care.
He is buried in clothing while
summer's still decomposing, but
he manages the heat and the stares.

The wobbly man serenades
street lamps at night 'til police
order him out of sight. He still
picks more flowers in the early
dew hours and hangs them where
they receive the most light.

FADING BEASTS & BUTTERFLIES

See: Its wings are losing their crystal.
They descend like broken glass on concrete,
color scattering from them like disintegrating
scales of dragons who still exhale hot fire
from dried out, allergy-ridden nostrils. Look,

if you hold the poor thing in your palm,
it tries to sleep without fluttering too much.
Its antennae twitch once, to signify uneasy
dreams with too many moving pictures.
There are castles to burn down during the night,
and butterfly effects to simulate. But earthquakes

don't start without metamorphosis, and
these small monarchs can't create history
without being able to fly. And dragons can't
incinerate evil warlocks if they can hardly breathe
on their own without inhalers built from stone,
their bodies shivering in a non-existent cold.

COMMUNITY PARK

There are endless corridors
of trees. They're stripped bare for now,
but they're pleading for you to
walk across the path they've forged
with their rooted feet.
They cherish the air you breathe.

Everywhere you turn here, they
wait for you - in self-made
Great Halls. Come sit a while,
they beckon, and have
a pint of ale or two. Your weary
bones deserve no less than
Mother Nature's clichéd comforts.

Because everything is colder now,
and the sting of wind invigorates you,
as the heat subsides in the face of fear.
The sun sleeps to avoid
incessant daytime nightmares.

And now - now that you've reached
the end of the path, the trees
wave goodbye to you. Their fingers
are puckered and stripped of color,
but once they blossom, you are
still welcome - even when they feel
beautiful enough not to require
your presence for their self-worth.

NEXT TUESDAY

My last honest effort
to find your little red-roofed cottage
in the middle of the charmed woods
ended with me scarred from a
bear attack and holding the skull
of a witch. Maybe you should

just meet me at the fork that veers
off into Nowhere's open mouth
or Somewhere's slippery palm.
Bring sandwiches, a water bottle,
and a light. It always gets dark
so fast when I want to visit you.

I SWEAR BY THESE WORDS

Save your breath for stories
worth the time. Shield your
eyes from monsters without glow.
Lantern oil does nothing when
you're blind. The heat will only
die out in your bones. Wish

upon a star before it dies. Dreams
get lost when they become black
holes. Try not to mind strangers'
wandering eyes. Wine is sweeter
when the moon is full. Drift

along your lifeline without
oars. Scars from your past will
be healed with age. Don't forget
to unlock all your doors, and don't
leave passion sleeping in a cage.

MAKE IT GAY

LESS TALKING

I have sacrificed
all verbosity of speech
to give you more time
to kiss me,
to touch me and unearth
the secrets beneath each
fold and wrinkle,

to trace an outline
around each scar
and stretch mark -
not to make constellations,
but to create
a whole new galaxy.
I have given up
the gift of the gab,
which was bequeathed to me
at Blarney Castle, where
the vertigo seized me
by the throat
as the tour guide clung
to my legs, and I

dangled
upside down,
seeing the world reversed
as if gravity would pull me
toward the clouds, into
the celestial halo, where
I would have met you
much sooner.

KISU SHITE-MO II?

For me, kissing a boy was like
driving to the local supermarket,
all cursive on the sign and rickety
automatic doors, and picking out
a plastic container of tuna rolls
from the sushi section, right next
to the artisanal cheeses and
the discounted wine display.

It tasted fine, for its price and
quantity. The dry rice was an adequate
vessel for the fish and avocado,
the seaweed slightly stiff before
giving in to the saliva and the
liquid hunger. Sometimes, the rolls
were meant to be spicy, though
I usually ached for a bottle of
sriracha to add some extra power
to a not-so-bold ensemble of flavors.

I thought that eating this stuff
for eight dollars was the best I
could get - something I could afford
and savor without scrutiny. Much like
boys' kisses, store bought sushi
leaves little to the imagination, but
at least I felt the ingredients were somewhat
thriving on my yearning tongue.

For me, kissing a girl was like
being seated at the bar in a small,
intimate restaurant, where the sushi
chefs offered an omakase, and I placed
my trust in the cuts of their salmon
and the art of their rolls. They made

me start light: thin sashimi drizzled
with delicate sauces, shrimp delivered
in squares on beds of rice and scallions.
As the plates got heavier, I could feel

the food dissolving in my mouth,
the blue crab leaving its savory
footprints on both my tastebuds
and my soul, the scallops scrambling
to make sense of my quivering
lips. Bite after bite, dish after dish, glass
after glass after glass of sake, I was warm,
comfortable, and at home. The personal
orgasm of culinary romance shook
me to my core and left me with pins
and needles and a lingering desire for
more (if only I had another hundred
dollars to spare for a second round).

Thankfully, kissing a girl doesn't require
a credit card. It gives you freedom in how
you choose from the menu provided in
that dimly lit izakaya on the corner of
downtown. You devour the hamachi,
sighing as it melts against your teeth,
tasting the tobiko as the shudders of
love start all over again before you even
get the chance to set your chopsticks down.

What I'm saying is that I love your sushi,
babe. And I will always eat your sushi.
I will eat the fuck out of your sushi. And
I'll always come back for seconds before
returning to that stupid grocery store
again for a package of mediocrity with
a side of Nirvana playing on the car stereo
and a sad puddle of gritty wasabi.

TAMBOURINE GAL

Heads up, everyone: It's the tambourine gal!
She's only in the band because of her boyfriend, you know.
He's the growly frontman with a heart made of gold,
and just as malleable, given she's probably a whore.

What's that? She's gay? Well, that's a pretty dyke!
Put up there to be aesthetically pleasing, I bet.
Sure, she can keep the rhythm and the tambourine a-jinglin',
but I bet she can't sing or play other instruments for shit.

What's that? Tambourine Gal plays the harp and the sax?
Well, who the fuck cares? I don't hear that on the tracks.
Oh, wait: There she is, on Side B. What a sound.
Though I'm sure she needed reverb for that sound to get around.

No? She's actually an incredibly talented musician?
Award-winning, prestigious, and with good pipes, too?
She did opera at Carnegie? Did duets with Bocelli?
Josh Groban as well? My god! What a surprising repertoire!

Does this mean that I have to recognize the tambourine gal
as being so much more than just a tambourine gal?
A musical delight and big dyke tambourine gal?
I think I'll buy a drink for the tambourine gal!

"Sorry, darling: I don't make time for people like you.
You who'd rather assume I'm worthless except for when I'm all a-jinglin."
Damn! Well, I got rejected, but I guess I had it comin'.
Let this be a lesson: Never doubt the tambourine gal!

NON-BINARY BARD FOR HIRE

Here's an idea for a brand new band:
Three enbies who can sing
and play strings. Power chords
and triplet goddamn harmonies
under a hot pink and blue flag
would totally be my thing.

This trans trio would tour every
major city and gay bar, suck down
AMFs and say adiós to the hating
motherfuckers down the street. One
of us will bust out the riffs, and then
the next tune will be crooned alongside
a cluster of ukes. Maybe we'll hire

someone to play synthesizer, but
only if they're super good and
super gender nonconforming. We'll
write underground, rainbow-tinged hits
like, "Sayonara, Cis Scum,"

"Back Home With the Homos," and
the ever catchy fan favorite, "What
I've Got Between My Legs." Spoiler
alert: We never tell you
what genitalia we have because
it's none of your fucking business!

We'll go through many names,
of course: Queer Quota,
Ultraviolet Spectrum, the Genderbenders.
We'll strut with our strumming, demi up
our drums, and be super fluid with

our favorite frantic fretting. We'll
perform love songs, booming ballads,
sad sonatas about broken hearts and
misunderstandings (transphobia sucks
just enough to sing about), all with

neon lights screaming in our hair
as the disco balls spin above our heads.
And of course, we'll make sure that at least
half our beats will boost endorphins and
get all the little gaybies to dance.

HIGH SCORE

The pretty girl who works
at the arcade just paid
for my grilled cheese sandwich
and my pink lemonade.

I'll race her on stationary motorcycles
and cars, twirl her hair like cotton candy
between my fingers. Does she want
a stuffed tiger, or a stuffed bear?

I'll impress her with my button
mashing on Street Fighter Whatever,
practice sharpshooting with a laser
gun and knock down every pixel.

I'll let her try out the game where
you gotta kill zombies with an
AK-47, and I think I'll let her win,
but she seriously kicks my ass.

I'll pay up to fifty dollars for these
games, just to see her smile. That
could buy me another four grilled
cheese sandwiches, sure, but it's

ninety degrees at the boardwalk,
the crowds are out, and inside,
the flashing lights and the clicking
pinball machines are the perfect

percussion. My stomach's roiling
from the dairy, but I still want
to play a game with the pretty
girl who works at the arcade.

THE RIGHT KIND OF CATCALLED

Borderline goddess
with Sailor Neptune hair
told me I was hot
from a driver's side pedestal.

All I could do
to express my gratitude
was say, "Thank you,"
while poorly saluting.

At least I didn't
imitate the Fonz
or stutter like I was cut
out of some chick flick popcorn shtick.

But I drove home
with a cackle on my tongue
and a high without Mary Jane
burning in my throat.

I called my wife
as soon as I could,
just to savor the moment
like a Girl Scout cookie.

And her reply
was just what I expected
(practically perfect in every way):
"She was absolutely right!"

NIGHT OUT

I planned to dance alone,
but that was before you came over
and swept me onto laminate floors
and kissed my hair with glitter lips.

I planned to just go home
after a drink or two,
but that was before you toasted
to my beauty and held my head up
when it felt too heavy.

Am I already falling in love
with a stranger in a torn denim
jacket and backwards snapback,
her tongue stamped with sweet rainbow
sherbet that melts just right in my mouth?

Or am I kidding myself,
and should I wait for the illusion
to subside until I, once again,
find myself on the dance floor alone?

HEART EYES

Two days ago,
my eyes assumed
the shape of hearts
after meeting
a beautiful girl.

It was rather painful,
and it was pretty scary.
The doctors told me,
however, that it
was only temporary.

I wore sunglasses
to hide it at first,
then averted my gaze
whenever she passed.

Then I saw the curves
around her pupils,
and the same subtle
trepidation, so I asked

if she would like a cup
of tea with me once
the percussion in my head
had finally subsided.

MAKE IT GAY

Got a fantasy saga of epic
daring in mind? Clashing swords
and drunken dwarves and cranky
dragons breathing fire? If you
don't want to fall into the trope
trap, there's a simple solution:
Make it gay. Your princess
and your knight should both be
honorable, yet badass dames.

Not writing fantasy? Perhaps
a western will sate your appetite.
Gunfights and saloon brawls
and sexy boa-wearing girls
may tickle your fancy. But hey,
make the sheriff and the deputy
both women who kiss after
dismounting their horses and
offing the evil outcast. Make it gay.

Or perhaps you want to craft
a space opera - something
deliciously sci-fi with ships
skipping like stones across
starlight. Well, why not have
a female alien swoon for a
cosmonaut nomad in a suit?
Make it gay. Space gays.
Gaaaaaays iiiiiin spaaaaaaace!

See, these genres are meant to
trigger creativity and ambition,
so be innovative and even avant-garde
with your authorial choices.
Make the plot twist more than a corkscrew.
Have the villain be the good guy all along.
Invent new languages and species
that are more than just reiterations
of elves and other creatures
that are always fucking white, why?!

Ahem. I digress. The world is
your oyster, and you ought to get
clever with how you show off your pearls.
But if there's anything I've learned, it's
to make it fun for the girls. Make them
fall in love. Make them one true pairing.
Make their pirate ship full masted while sailing.
Keep the fanart and fanfiction from staling.
Make it gay.

DATE NIGHT AT THE GAY BAR

Look at her go,
feet all tip tapping to the rhythm,
as the amateur artist keeps rapping
about his mom and "brand new crib"
that's probably just a studio in the worst
part of town. Though to be fair, in this
economy, he's got it fucking made.

But look at her go.
She smiles like lightning bolts, wears
silver like it's part of her skin, stretches
her fingers into spider web tattoos along
my back, and I am so. Fucking. Here
for that nonsense.

There are rainbows everywhere.
All the way down to the sponsorship
signs, we are glowing in neon vodka
bottles and beer spigots. We are wearing
snapbacks and bowling shirts. We are
avoiding the dykes with top buns,
even though they're trying so hard
to make them look good.

She loves to dance,
and so do I - I just blow hard, calcified
chunks at it. But she pulls me under
the laughter of the disco ball, and we
spin with rum and cider bubbling
in our vintage systems. And while
we don't kiss, we get so, so close.

LESBIAN SAILORS

The beautiful sirens can't be dodged:
not even lesbian sailors can resist.
They're enticed by hoodies and beanies
and saying, "I love you," after the first kiss.

Watch the captain in her crisp uniform
fall prey to the sirens' call: "Oh, lass,
swim to my rock where I've perched,
and I'll rent us both a U-Haul."

"We'll adopt two dogs - big ones!"
they cry. "A Rottie and a Pit Bull!
And we'll go bowling every Friday night
while I suck away your soul."

But one smart lesbian sailor - what luck -
can hear but endure the hype.
"Sorry, ladies," she declares to the sirens scared.
"I don't fall prey to stereotypes."

HOCUS POCUS

She pivots against my hips,
her lips set to a rolling boil,
the contents of my stomach roiling
in a fermented abyss of drunk bliss.

Oh, sweet sorceress, her spells
are of the physical - the way she
bends my body without breaking
my spirit, the way
she contorts my frame without
warping the picture held
within it. She flexes me,
while she hexes me.

The heat! The heat! The ever
swarming heat. It's a good heat,
an enchanted heat. The trick is in
the gyrations, the magic in the
touch. We'll guzzle our brew
together, soften
our swollen palates, the taste
subdued only by stars, sprinklings
of dust escaping from the pages
of her curious, furious tome.

ROMANCEBOT XOXOXO

Fell in love with an android
who had the body of a superstar
and the brain of a philosopher.
She'd read books faster than I
could take them off the shelf. She
did not eat, but she said my cooking
smelled, in her words, divine.

Fell in love with an android
who saved me on a street corner
one night when I was too drunk
to walk in a straight line. She
pulled me back from the crosswalk
before a pick-up truck sent my
torso one way and my legs another.

Fell in love with an android
who carried me to bed every night,
who sang me lullabies and never got
the notes wrong, yet still sounded as
natural as a diva sighing out an aria.
When she lay next to me, her heating
and cooling systems did wonders for
my sleep during the heat waves and
The cold snaps. Her kisses were soft.

I fell in love with someone
who was more humanoid than all
the men and women I let tattoo
their names on my heart. This one
didn't brand me. She made sure
I could be built from stuff as tough
as she was. And when I cried, she
made me tea. And when I laughed,
she smiled. And when I dreamed,
she hummed and whirred and buzzed
like a serene blue silicon sea.

ÉIRE, 2010

When I was twenty years old, I drank
myself stupid in a Dublin hostel. I saw
constellations I didn't think existed before in
the walls' withering yellow plaster. Scars

grew in a night sky's perfect throat, and
I could hear muffled music beneath my
mattress. No rhythm, though. No cadence.
Made it easier to sleep. Breakfast the next

day was dry toast - no jam. I was left to
wallow in a green morning because it can
get very green in Ireland, stereotypical
imagery be damned. To think I couldn't

have fallen in love there, in love with
a girl who could play the banjo or accordion
instead of a fiddle or a flute. Nothing flimsy,
something sturdy, her fingers stamped with

calluses. Sprite and vodka and cider and
one mouthful of Guinness carried me to
unsteady sleep, and I was twenty years old
when I flew back from Limerick a week

earlier than I anticipated. To think if I had
stayed. To think if I had known. To think
if I had sung another tired traditional tune
until scars formed in my throat, too.

YOUR BODY IS FULL OF STARS

Sit still for a moment so I can count them:
All of your brown constellations, the cosmos
burned into your skin in scattered dark spots
like an opening into a new dimension.

When you breathe, I can count them, all
of them, like the swirling of a galaxy. Your
spirals spin across your belly, your asteroid
belt tattooed against your hips. Your arms
and face expose horoscopes you can't find

in newspapers. An omen on your chin - celestial
advice dotting your cheeks - a sign of health
and fortune mottled like cinnamon on
the bridge of your nose. Your body is full

of stars, and while sometimes, I see
your speckles and freckles as merely "cute,"
other nights, you cover me in your nebulae,
conceal me in your night sky, hold me close
to your burning breath until we both fall
into the erupting supernova.

RELIGIOUS TRAUMA

THE HUMAN SEMINAR

There is nothing sinister
about how I present myself.
I am all shapes. I am all sizes.
I am not all colors, though. One
shade is all I provide, and shade
is far different than shadow.

I rely heavily on poise:
the way I place my feet, the way
I fold my fingers together
like origami, the way I project
my voice across a room.

I'm like a human bullhorn, rattling
and piercing and set to the wrong
volume. It's a cumbersome task
to enact a successful demonstration
of fact and reasonable fiction.

Sometimes, I pretend
I am not actually here. The world
becomes a soft ball of clay,
or silly putty, reminding me
of the dirty fingernail days
of my childhood,

the days in which I swallowed
pebbles as if consuming
miniature galaxies - harder
than stars. But somehow,
more brittle, too. Back then,
I didn't care how many people
witnessed the irrationality
of my early eating habits.

God knows they expect me now
to stomach less edible things.
I'd rather be a toddler chewing rocks
and drinking mud like a milkshake
through a bendy straw than
a pretentious bastard gnawing
on the gristle of his own words.

Sometimes, I pretend
I am not actually here. That
I am not in front of an impatient
audience of few. When I
can hold my universe against
my palms and warm it up,

everything becomes delightfully
disconnected. Because
the presentation is now over. The
performance has come to a close. And
I will not be taking any questions.

ROOM 108

Within this dreary corridor,
the odor from Room 108
entices me: Baked bread,
dried rosemary, Catholic mass
incense and hot perspiration.
Garlic to ward away vampires.
Hydrogen sulfide to polish silver.
I never knock, however, and I
return to my own den in carpeted
silence. I drink old brandy and read
the leatherbound Gideon Bible.
I dream of kissing Gideon.
I dream of fucking Esther.

In those dreams, Room 108
also becomes a classroom, one
that I cannot teach or learn in.
There are whiteboards with
runes inscribed into them. Scratched
into them.

And all the children circle
one chair where the stories told
have teeth. So does the light
at the end of the corridor.

Where the Eagles play that same
song. Where it feels all too familiar.

Where you last kissed Gideon
and slipped your fingers into Esther
and used acrylic nails
to strip my soul away.
And you sleep soundly
in a queen-size bed
in Room 108.

SURVIVOR'S GUILT

Here,
kneeling on a diamond studded shore,
I watch the separated smiles
float past me. In the foam,
they pretend to cope with demons.

Each ray of evening sun
catches teeth not yet broken,
yet they are clenched, and pinched,
and ground into dust that holds
the consistency of a dead man's ash.

I am lucky
that I was able to swim to land.
The rip tide pulled everyone else
away - and here I am,
making it all about me and not
the bubbles floating from their last breath.

Here,
I find myself to be an illusion -
not a survivor, but a fake phantom,
looming behind the curtains of
red impostor syndrome,
dreading the day I must be dragged
back down beyond the reef and held
accountable for my sins.

THE GRAVITY OF IT ALL

No matter how many times I told myself
that I wouldn't screw this up, here we are:

Standing in the middle of a black hole
where a house used to be. Tornado Alley.

Shreds of watercolor family portraits
everywhere. The cat survived, thank God.

At least he'll find a good second home
with your in-laws, and I'll sit under the shade

of a birch tree, which has pollen that I'm highly
allergic to, and I'll sneeze out all my sins.

There won't be a day that goes by that I don't
wish for a time machine to go back and clock

my past self repeatedly in the jaw. Fuck TMJ:
this will hurt a lot more, linger a lot longer.

This will teach you not to dance with hypotheticals
dressed up in ball gowns and pearl necklaces.

This will teach you not to serenade badly written
thesis statements with a formerly six string guitar.

Five strings don't cut it here, boss. Neither do
five bruised hearts. Not broken, bruised.

You can't break hearts because they're too sturdy,
but the contusions take a really fucking long time to fade.

They say that not even light can escape from a black hole.
Is that why there wasn't a sunrise after you left?

CONCERNS RE: POTENTIAL AFTERLIFE

Tell me, Lord, how will
you greet me once I am dead?
Will you be dressed
in your Sunday best,
or will you have just
rolled out of bed?

Will you meet me instead in
your office where the shades
are drawn against Heaven's skies?
Will you look deep into my eyes?
Maybe eye contact isn't exactly
your cup of tea. Or more aptly,
your brimming cup of wine.

Tell me, are there gardens
to tend to where you reside?
Is there both sun to bask under
and fog in which to hide?

Perhaps I will find you standing
on the bridge that connects you
to the world you shaped with
your warm, bare hands. Below
us, a beach to walk on, where
we'll burn our feet on the sand.

You will not carry me this
time, Lord. Now we can roam
side by side. Only trust me
when I tell you that I'll never
be ready to die.

POIGNANCY IS DEAD

I will not go too deep;
the imagery
that compels me to watch sunsets
is strictly the color, not the limit
of my existence.

To focus on such mortality
is to steer a train through the convulsing tunnels
of my mind.

Monsters like to live in mansions,
not sewers. They chew more
on the silverware than the food
said silverware is meant to spear.

I could spew more commentary
like acid reflux as if I have something
potent to say.

But only my throat burns,
not my words. And so,
I will not go too deep.

I thought I could fight a bear.
But the bear was already wounded.
Its fur bore Death's constellations
in red and gray cosmic woe.

It spoke to me in English:
"You're trying too hard on these metaphors.
Sometimes, a bear is a bear.
A sunset is a sunset.
Heartburn is heartburn.
And dust is dust."

THE ANGRY, VIOLENT, & SOMEWHAT HORNY AGNOSTIC'S PRAYER

Oh, Great Whatever,
grant me the strength to forgive
my enemies for being complete
douchenozzles, so that I may go
to sleep on time without fretting
over which kitchen utensil I will
use to stab them in the eyes.

Vengeance is a cruel mistress,
but she's good in bed, and she
knows how to win an argument.
I'll need your Some Such Spirit
to pacify me before I set my
foes' houses on fire.

This is my humble prayer.
Amen, motherfuckers.

CATHOLICISM, CRYSTALS, & CUNNILINGUS

We met while sitting in the same pew
as our cousins took their first communion.
Meanwhile, our Eucharist was much sweeter
and certainly came with more than a sip of wine.

Years later, I decided that staring at my fragmented
soul in stained glass wasn't my cup of tea,
so I bought books on witchcraft and drew
symbols of hope and love and healing
in the dirt just outside our little house.

She ultimately shirked the rosary, too,
so now we have tea time over tarot cards,
celebrate the equinox with friends, and
sleep soundly with dreams more focused on
redwoods than red mea culpa lashes.

THE DEVIL'S COOL WITH THIS

Someone once told me
to kiss her ass and go to Hell.
I said to her, "If that's the case,
I'll have to scorch your little tush
with my big, burning lips." She
surprisingly was impressed, and
she offered me a bourbon.

Two hours later, we were drunk
and making out in her tiny bedroom
overlooking the overpass in a shitty
part of town where the rats had evolved
faster than the humans had. And once
she pulled me to the bed, she whispered
in my ear, "Guess what, sweetheart:

You get to kiss my ass, and now
we'll both go to Hell in a handbasket."
And so the fiery chariot was built
below our feet, waiting to carry us
to Satan's sauna, while for the time
being we heated up each other's bodies
with our mouths and tongues, sipping
the air like nectar stolen from Heaven.

SINNAMON BUNS

Your fingers are so sticky, sticky, sticky -
they cling to the Virgin Mary's hands,
and she licks away the frosting lingering
on your smooth milk chocolate fingers.

Breakfast is served for saints and sinners
alike, but the buns are yours alone.
Squeeze them for good measure before
you place your mouth atop their peaks.

For thine is the kingdom and power of Heaven,
and thine is the sweetness and tang of the Lord.
And Mary is eager to invite you over
for seconds when her son Jesus isn't looking.

For thine is the kingdom and power of Heaven,
and thine is the sweetness and tang of the Lord.
He'll let you sprinkle sugar on the back of his mistress,
who will kiss you and stick to you when Christ isn't looking.

THE GALLERY

God dipped Their fingers
into a basin of blue paint,
but even They
could not change the hues
of reds and yellows
and oranges.

They could not smell
the smoke, but God knew
it was there - trapped somewhere
between Heaven and the Earth,
the two constants from the beginning
now swathed in too warm of blankets.

Below, sensing eternal inferno,
mortals cried out, "Hellscape!
Apocalypse! End times!"
And all God could do
was smear the oils
onto a blank canvas of clouds,
close Their eyes, and pray
to someone more supreme than Themself.

BOOZY PROG ROCK DANCE NUMBER

This inescapable ennui
holds as much strength
as a dessert cocktail usurping
the sobriety throne at 9:30 PM.
It helps that it's sweet, without
punching down.

It's all short walks and worries
for me - the termination of a
wheel's turn, before the automobile
spits me out on the curb beside
downtown. I drink in the warm
evening air as if taste testing
a liqueur I've never tried.

I guess I have always been
intrigued by the ordinary.

They say God would be an alcoholic
if he crash landed on Earth like
a reluctant Superman. Given his son's
conniptions over watered down wine,
I wouldn't be surprised. He waits

until Mother Mary isn't looking,
then slips a shot of bourbon into
a short glass of ice water. It's
tamped down, but the bite is there.
It nibbles rather than snaps,
but it's still there.

And I, I have a scraped ankle
caught in the rope trap of ennui.
It pulls me up to Genesis's rainbows,
to Rael's name sprayed above the
lamb lying down on Broadway, and
I am envious of his alleged enlightenment -
if only because my life would be a little
more interested and a lot less overwhelming.

TAROT READING

Come, chariot, come,
and unload this burden from my back.
My eyes are faced forward,
but my shoulders ache from the strain.

Sleep, lion, sleep.
You are inner strength tamed
and led by a loose chain. Your dreams
will only be disrupted should the devil tempt
me into self-enslavement
once again. See the world

in all its triumph. There, she tiptoes
and reaches equilibrium. She dances,
and the water kisses her ankles. She twirls
her batons, and the silver matches the light
of the moon above. See: I think I am

unworthy of the accolades I receive,
for I do not consider myself a Renaissance
man, nor do I find my skills honed enough
to make me a master of any design. But
the light crowns my head as well as any
bejeweled diadem, and I can be as much
a queen or king as all other monarchs
before me.

Rest, chariot, rest,
and let me recover my senses for a while.
The sun rises and sets over this year,
and Chaos is given a blanket to swaddle
its children in and a pillow to rest its head on.
Pan is horned, but disoriented. His vision
is not as good these days. I set my load
down for another day. Above me are

the silhouettes of those who sacrificed
their lives while still enjoying livelihood.
They offer me the wand, the sword,
the pentacle, and the cup. I drink, and I am
nourished. The blade is resolute on my hip.
I let the fireworks stream and the glow of new
success guide me. I have an agenda of
my own. I must tend to it, if

I wish to see my hopes come into fruition.
I wish, above all else,
to be the Magician.

SURREALISM AND THE STARS

The fissure I thought was in
my engagement ring was, in fact,
in my finger, and when I pinched
the white fibers sprouting from the gash,
I pulled out strip after strip of sticky brie.
A Salvador Dalí diagnosis in the making.

Before I had the dream in which
I yanked dairy from my dangling flesh,
I held you in my arms and wondered aloud
what it would be like to be a star with you,
to live for millions of years, watching
the universe through cosmic, intangible eyes,
only to explode in a glorious, rosy fire
and become something else entirely -
a white dwarf, or a majestic black hole.

"Maybe," I had murmured, "ironically,
it's when we die that we become truly
immortal. That we become stardust
and remain a vibrant shard of a constantly
expanding universe, forever."

Yet despite the poignancy, I dreamed
about tugging cheese in gooey rectangles
out of a hole in my hand instead. Sometimes,
even after an overly pretentious display of
human speculation over things unknown,
my subconscious does me a solid and ropes
me back into the world of the absurd that
I have grown so accustomed to living in,
whether fast asleep,
or wide, wide awake.

SACRAMENT

And, just like that,
I hear the fluttering
of wings accompanying
the church bells,

and as I raise my head from
weeping, all around me,
white origami bodies cast shadows
on stained glass flashbacks

before warbling sacrilegiously
toward the abandoned altar. There,
Christ dips his toes in wine.
He eats the remaining bread
that wasn't sanctified. He watches
the doves fight for light
beyond the arch, and with
a smile aimed at me, he opines,

"Peace always finds difficulty
reaching the outside
of a gold-coated man's prayer
and a cathedral built from lies."

WE LIVE IN A SOCIETY

WELCOME, FRIEND

When they shut the door
in your face, go ahead
and read the map I provided
you in the forest, and if
the mist lifts, you will find
my door is wide open.

It is dark, and cold, and scary
outside, and there are beasts
leaving angry welts of footprints
in the sludge. But keep your
lantern lit and your companions close,
and you'll find my cabin soon enough.

There, I will stoke the fire,
pour enough tea to sate your
sense of abandonment, and tell
stories to a lilting song until
you sleep in the amber glow
of lost nostalgia laced with
a faint licorice hint of hope.

HELLO, SUNNY

Sunny was born with a chance
to catch the sky before it fell in Texas.
She held onto a piece with both hands
and let the blisters linger for days.

Sunny was eleven when she found her
father in the back of his pick-up truck
with another man. They both bore scars
from separate car accidents on their chests.
Their fingers left marks on each other's skin.

Sunny fell in love when she was seventeen
and had her heart broken when she was eighteen.
She forged for herself a spine of steel
and learned to shrug off the cudgel's blows.

Sunny was ready to die in the arms of her
fiancée when the bombs started dropping in
Dallas. They said World War III ended with
a scorched kiss on the top of Earth's head.
Sunny let her own lips melt away, too.

But none of that matters, because Texas lacks
pockmarks from nuclear annihilation, and
the sky is intact and as blue as ever above us,
and we all know that Sunny isn't real.

BLESS THE BONES OF CALIFORNIA

These days are getting short enough
to chew on. You can feel the sunsets
swelling right on your molars, melting
like butter in between your lips. On the side

of the road, a dirt scarred truck
sits on a lopsided slope. One headlight
is gouged out, like a wandering eye
ripped out of its metal socket.

Deep in the fields of Cotati,
you can drink the September heat
like soup still in its can, the salt boiled
away, leaving only the cream to scald
your mouth after the first sip. Only a few

neighborhoods away, the fires have taken
everything. Our relatives are left with
silhouettes of ash, but we still have
our house, our two acres, our banalities.

I can hear your boots assault the
skeletons of leaves on the patio outside. I am
old enough to understand the profanity
that you use to button up your
one-size-too-small shirt.
You are young enough to still carry me

on your shoulders, but once it gets dark
too quickly, your shadow weighs
us both down, and the North Bay swallows
us up in its maw until the sunrise
is cool enough to eat with a spoon.

POST-JENTACULAR

After a light breakfast
of lemon poppy seed scones
and jasmine crème brûlée tea,

I took a walk down to the shopping
plaza, where the pirate man had
washed ashore and was hunched
over on his stone perch,

counting sheep in daylight
as he pondered over the plight
of his people, left alee and
making friends with the Kraken.

It was clearer than the sky
above my head that he was
making up his own hymns.

Prayers for people who didn't
look like me but suffered ten
times more than I could ever
imagine. They bled while I breathed.

Meanwhile, a group of friends
played an outside DnD session,
their D20's glittering beneath the
wheels of Helios's chariot.

In front of me, a young man moved
to the hip hop throbbing from the speaker
on his hip, while he also
wore a tiny, iridescent kid's backpack.

Another man held up a sign outside
the grocery store, brow thick
and furrowed like a serpent burrowed
amid the sand, a baseball cap

leaving a tattoo on his forehead.
"Defund the Police," the crooked
sharpie ordered, and the old carts
whistled by him, all eyes forward.

With a stained glass heart, I passed him,
thanked him, loudly agreed with him.
It didn't matter. I was a bard, not a warrior.

How "nice" of me to assume such a role.
I would not wear bruises like bracelets.
I would not be zip-tied, carted into
a van like I was nothing but cattle.

On the way back home, I saw six children
chasing one another with sticks in
the courtyard. One of them had a remote control
racecar. It was bright red, with a white stripe.

It zipped by me and disappeared behind
a tree stump. It left no trace behind.
I guess we had that in common.

The children complimented me on my
hair. My wife's was prettier, though. Pink
versus purple. Very important to think about.
Now my stomach was rumbling again.

SOUTHAMPTON

He wears white socks and black croc
sliders because they're comfortable, and he
doesn't give a damn what the bystanders think.
His purple jacket gives him Prince vibes,
and that's all that matters to him.

On the asphalt steps, he counts Tetris
blocks on his phone, but the puzzle
he started in his apartment remains dusty.
Meanwhile, the aesthetically pleasing couple -
the man in torn jeans, black leather,
wide-brimmed hat; the girl with ebony hair,

sweet shades, pink lips, and a mix of husky
and chihuahua on her lap - rub each other's
backs and sip coffees and chais. It's all a
suburban game in the end, my friend: It's all
a stupid little suburban game.

THE DRAGONFLIES IN BENICIA

The dragonflies in Benicia
are painted blue
and red and green
dipping their wings
into the marina
where the boats wear
their strange names
like medals of honor
on their spines

Two women walk down
to the salt-addled pier
They let the wind carry
them halfway there
and avid fishermen
let their hooks catch clouds
that have grown fins
in the deepest part
of the murky strait

It's enough to stare
into antique shops
but not buy anything
It's enough to sample
mint chip milkshakes
on a cold evening
It's enough to get
a taste of small town
decorum so you can
finally understand exactly
what all the fuss is about

The retired become artists
to replace the artists
who have retired
and somewhere, cities
are still on fire, while
a regime swallows up
more territory without
needing a fork or knife

but you can ignore that
if it bothers you
or it gets under your collar
and itches like hives
Instead, you can watch
the dragonflies flutter
across the god rays
in the sky just above
your new suburban life

UPPER HAPPY HILLS

The rain looks like whiplash
on the window. The train treads
water - new rubber boots, new steel,
new hooves and horseshoes, forged and fitted,
leaving bruises on rust in the Upper Happy Hills.

Tell me, are there Lower Happy Hills
that people reside in? And if so, do they
smile more than their northern neighbors? Do they

whistle brighter tunes and carry lighter loads,
wearing no scars on their shoulders
after bearing the temporary burden?
Do they tie raindrops across their throat like

vaporous cloaks, and once the storm subsides,
protection fades as quickly as sunlight staining
the roofs of their mouths like molten glass?

And is the noise not as grating
on ears carved out of brittle limestone? And if
they erode, are they reformed as gods or slaves?
Do golems scream louder than children with

crossed legs and blackened knees do, perched
like parrots on the curved mustached lip of
the dark and dusty Upper Happy Hills?

73 FLOORS UP

We see the urban world revealed
in black and white comic strips
all panels still in motion
the characters dealing with
their personalized dilemmas
with text bobbing above
their heads and speech bubbles
losing their fraying borders

We are condensed into newsprint
puzzles and cryptograms
We pretend to see everything
in color when there is no more
saturation in the air
If we look closely at the view
the boats on the gray water
stop moving just long enough
to blend into the background
just like graphite disintegrating
into smudged and faded shadows

We see everything revealed
as flat instead of elevated
as dim instead of bright
Maybe in the dead of night
we will notice a different hue
but that is only if the artist
feels like changing the palette
of an old, forgotten city

THE LAST MOUNTAINEER

At last, I scale the pinnacle
of a city that houses only
shadows on its canvas: The
steel artwork, the twists and bends
of human fever. I paint smiles on
faces with no teeth; they cannot
chew the gristle of lost time. If
all I have left is one color, I will
splash it onto the pulsing skin
of a skyscraper. Each window
lights up like night terror eyes.
Below me, the commuters are
clustered in clouds of smoke.
Their movement is impermanent.
Their lips hold back words as fine
as unraveling strings. On this metal
peak, I view everything. And yet,
I see nothing I didn't already know.

METROPOLIS NOW

The city is one big metallic bruise,
a hematoma that this country could
never recover from. The purple smog

and the blackened skies do wonders
for the stomachs of the citizens
stumbling to their morning posts,

which, exhaustingly, are the same
as their evening posts. Exciting.

The paper boys are as thin as
the print they sell, and as dark,
too. They keep pyrite under their

caps, so the wolves don't bite -
they don't have the appetite for
fool's gold. Distant relatives

pound notes on typewriters
in an effort to recreate music
from another generation. The text

is taut and stressed. No amount
of singing can ease this anxiety. The
city stays a sore sight in even the warmest

glow. Ice will only cool down a feverish
head. It won't draw the demons out.

A KING UNCROWNED

Look, Mommy! Look how they
sanitize the preacher in handcuffs! They've
poured bleach across his back, attempted
to whitewash him like a picket fence, and
stripped his skin of the vibrancy of his
nature. What will they do to him now?

You see, dear, they will reform him.
Bend his back into an endless arc of their
own self-righteousness. They will yank
his tongue out of his mouth and make him
slur platitudes that will appease the mob,
who will now praise this new scrubbed soul
and feel better about themselves. They

will scrawl his safest quotations on statues
and classroom walls. They will share his least
controversial decorum to the palest children. They
will speculate on how he'd react to dissent were
he alive a century or so from now. As if
the hollowed out shell they've destroyed would
yield to them like broken bigots' puppetry. A man
created in their own image, rather than his own.

Son, watch how they ferment his legacy:
they shall parade him around the town square,
his head held up as if by an invisible noose.
They shall shriek about his dream until the
words have lost all meaning. They will pluck
the bullet from his breast, hold it up so that
the sun catches the red of his blood, and cry,

"Look - see how he died for us! See how he
died for love and peace! And see how you
feel so much better echoing the lines that
cleanse you of your sin, without the need
to change your behavior, or your family,
or your town, or the very system we hold dear.

"So let's teach the philosophy of being nice
to one another, and let's complain when no one
can get along! No matter the grievance, tell
them to keep their heads down, because we're
all the same in the end, aren't we? We're all
the same in the end. We're all the same
in the end."

DISCOVERY PHASE

Distant from the truth,
I dredge up the past
between my stained fingers
like spoiled white flour.
This quick heart of mine
beats incessantly, as if
it will make the memories
less inedible. But I still can't
eat them. They will sit
like boulders in my stomach.

This post-fact world
is lopsided, derailed,
shaped like forgotten cargo.
You live in it with me, but
I have difficulty counting
the words shared between us
without a broken abacus.
I've forgotten how to say, I love you,
because I've been told it no longer
means what I want it to mean.

Nearly seven years ago,
while sitting on a red couch,
I exposed everything in my chest
to a professional without a face.
I don't remember her face. Her
eyes were black holes sucking in
every ounce of debris that I
scattered from my shoes. Now
I'm not sure if the insomnia
that once wrapped around me
like hotel sheets was real
or a prolonged fever dream.

Because every star above
my head already died tens
of millions of years ago, and all
light gets separated between
the lips of skyglow. The bed
I sleep on is not made out of
springs, but numbers pulled from
a false god's data bank. And we're all
part of some bullshit simulation,
anyway, so who cares if I say,
I love you, fifty times in one night
to you, since you won't
actually hear it even once?

THE WALTZ

The tension is so thick in
this silver-bloated ballroom
that you'd have to cut it
with a blowtorch and serve it
seared on the top to the nearest glutton
in attendance. And yet, here we

are: I take your hand, and you spin
your hips into my sides, leaving
divots in my skin. I can't remove
the offending dents, but I can
decorate them, cover them
with hood ornaments so that I

retain a little value once I'm
inevitably taken to the junkyard
and ground into a fine dust.
The men wear tuxedos that adhere
to their frames like a penguin's
feathers. The women have dipped
their arms up to their elbows

in tapestries woven from pure gold,
so they can't lift their kerchiefs
to their swollen mouths because their hands
are weighed down. You and I, in blue
and green, ought to be put on display
in a shop somewhere, to be driven off

the lot by voyeurs desperate to observe
just how we function together. How we
run. How we synchronize. How we rev
up each other's engines so well. Funny
how our bodies repel each other like
static electricity on alloy, but if it
gets hot enough, the pianist will

have to abandon the melting ebonies
and ivories, and like fiberglass,
we'll bend toward each other once again,
locking lips and not even wincing
at the sight or sensation of the blisters
rising in a reddened infinity sign.

SPRAY PAINT & PERFUME

Because you like to smell nice when
you tag the nearest crumbling city hall,
you soak your soul in tangerine and
cherry watermelon bliss. By the end

of the night, the mix of citrus and formaldehyde
gives you the odor of someone who died
and was embalmed in the middle of a fucking
orchard. Though sometimes, you do switch

to the forest fumes or the vanilla sugar
sweetness, the sticky scent wafting
from under your black hoodie as you
evade police who do not take kindly
to your portrait of the mayor with

his head buried so far up his own ass
that he doesn't need to get a colonoscopy
after all. Personally, my favorite is the
cologne that strangely burns like coffee
on your skin - the bitter bean overpowers

the chemical sterility crooning
from your aerosol can, leaving red
and blue streaks across concrete cheeks
that needed make-up on their graying
bones. Like a painter hunched over an easel
in the dead end corner of a hole-in-the-wall

café, your splattered self is great
for cuddles, while the sirens howl past
our apartment, never finding you. Never
finding us. Never compromising our art.

THE AFTERMATH

We are temporary ghosts
suspended in nectar,
full of fireworks and running rivers.
We taste sweet,
we weep in reservoirs,
and we explode in the most
colorful ways.

If the gods gave us a chance
to live forever, who knows
how many of us would take
the chance. After a while,
our fingers would fray like
old fabric - strings
dangling
from cuticles, hangnails
that cannot be cut
without tempting the Fates.

Is it enough for us
to dream of endless youth?
We have learned to fly,
learned to heal,
learned to cope with mortality.
But the fountain that Ponce sought
was never full of anything
drinkable.
It was full of sand,
and Time sifted it
between Her teeth.

www.ingramcontent.com/pod-product-compliance
Lightning Source LLC
Chambersburg PA
CBHW070435010526
44118CB00014B/2055